A closer LOOK at ESKIMOS

Jill Hughes

Illustrated by
Maurice Wilson

Hamish Hamilton · London

Inuit: the people

The Eskimo people, 75,000 of them today, are scattered from Greenland to eastern Russia: a distance of more than 9,500 kilometres. Until the nineteenth century, the Eskimo were almost completely undisturbed by the world beyond the ice. They lived as nomadic hunters, moving their snow or stone and turf houses and skin tents with the seasons in search of game, which they killed with weapons of bone, ivory or wood.

The first white adventurers coming to the 'frozen north' told tales of a land of ice and snow, a barren wilderness without trees and, in the winter, even without sun. The Eskimo saw, and sees, his land very differently. To him it is always alive, changing subtly with the six seasons of his year. The Eskimos, who call themselves *Inuit*, 'the people', are tough and skilful hunters. Until very recently, what they could kill had to provide them with all the

Mongoloid features
With their broad cheeks and slanting eyes, Eskimos bear a close resemblance to the races of north-east Asia. Their eyes show the Mongoloid fold — which may have developed to protect the eyes against snow glare.

Eskimo groups
The origins of the Eskimo people are unknown but the earliest inhabitants of the far north were probably an Asiatic inland people. When the climate became colder, the population shifted to the sea. The first coastal peoples hunted seal and walrus. They were followed by a wave of whale hunters who spread eastwards from Asia along the northern coast. The Eskimos in the west show a complex mixture of Eskimo and Indian or Asiatic customs. The groups of the eastern Arctic lie furthest from contact with southern life. Some Canadian Eskimos, particularly the Netsilik, Caribou and Igloolik groups, were still living as partially nomadic hunters, moving from one seasonal camp to another until the 1950s. Many of their customs had existed since the thirteenth century.

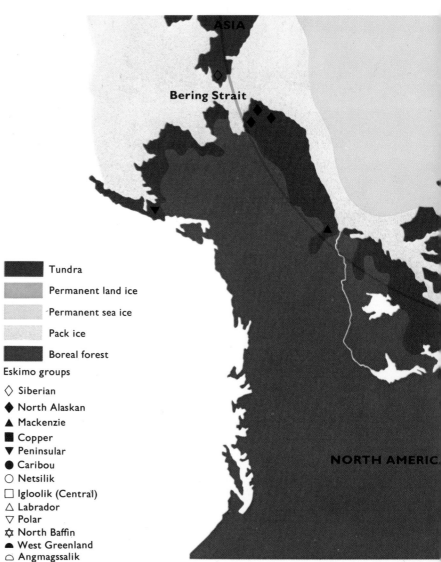

Tundra
Permanent land ice
Permanent sea ice
Pack ice
Boreal forest

Eskimo groups
◇ Siberian
◆ North Alaskan
▲ Mackenzie
■ Copper
▼ Peninsular
● Caribou
○ Netsilik
□ Igloolik (Central)
△ Labrador
▽ Polar
✿ North Baffin
◖ West Greenland
◠ Angmagssalik

ASIA
Bering Strait
NORTH AMERICA

necessities of life: food, clothing, shelter, transport and fuel. Each group had its own way of life, largely decided by the kind of animals it hunted and the sort of terrain it inhabited.

The Eskimos of Alaska and Greenland are separated by vast distances but united by a basically similar language, in some of their habits and beliefs, and by many of the animals they hunt. Being able to live off the land of the Arctic is not the only special mark of the Eskimo. Most of their people have traditionally lived in small groups of a few families. They have often had to rely on each other for survival and are always dependent on the people around them for comfort and company. As a result, the Inuit have tended to be cheerful, considerate and generous. Although many of the features of traditional Eskimo life described in these pages have vanished, these characteristics of the Inuit have survived.

Arctic circle

GREENLAND

Hudson Bay

People of the past
These statuettes, of walrus ivory, were discovered in Greenland. They were made in about AD 900 by people of the Eastern Dorset Culture who preceded the Eskimo. They seem to have merged with the Eskimo in the east of Greenland.

The face of the Arctic
The Eskimos live in an Arctic climate even though most of them live outside the Arctic circle. Winters are long and severe with up to four months when the sun stays below the horizon. Summers are cool with long periods of continuous daylight. The majority of Eskimos live north of the tree line. Inland lies the tundra, vast plains of stunted grass, heather and lichen which grow on top of permanently frozen sub-soil called permafrost. The Arctic coastline is varied, with low-lying tundra, rocky outcrops, and coastal cliffs, or alpine mountains. In most areas where Eskimos live, the sea is a fertile mixture of the Arctic Ocean and the warmer waters of the Atlantic or the Pacific. It is rich in fish and plankton which attract large numbers of seal, walrus and whale. The bays and straits of the rugged coast are frozen solid in winter and make good hunting grounds for sea mammals and highways for sledge travel.

The seasonal round

The Arctic is not perpetually covered in a thick blanket of ice and snow. Although above the tree line, where most Eskimos live, the temperature rarely rises above 15°C, dramatic seasonal changes take place that affect all life there – including the Eskimos. Six seasons are distinguished by the Eskimo hunters: early and late spring, summer, autumn, and early and late winter. People who depend on hunting for survival have to be attuned to the changing seasons and know what sort of weather and what animal life they bring. The Eskimo language contains a large number of words for different kinds and states of snow and ice: an indication of the vital part the weather plays in Eskimo life.

Most Eskimos live on the coast, and winter is passed on or at the edge of the sea ice where there is always a supply of food, fuel and material for clothing in the shape of the seal. Warm in their sod and stone, or snow, houses, the Eskimos can hunt seal at breathing holes even in the depths of winter. Seals have to surface regularly to breathe and Eskimo hunters learn to find the breathing holes under their covering of snow. They can use dog sledges to cross the thick ice, travelling long distances if necessary, in search of seal, trapping foxes, and occasionally finding a polar bear.

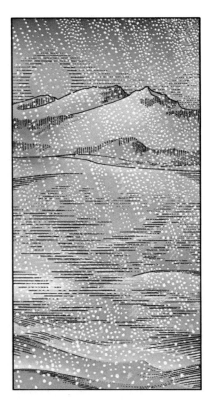  

Early spring (March–April)
There are heavy snowfalls but the sun appears. Eskimos hunt seals at breathing holes and may shoot an occasional caribou.

Late spring (May–July)
Days are at their longest. The snow begins to melt. Families move into summer tents. Seals are hunted on the ice edge.

Summer (August–September)
Eskimos move inland to hunt birds, fish and gather berries. On the coast they hunt sea mammals. The first snow falls.

In summer, the dogs can be used as pack animals, winter houses are exchanged for sealskin or caribou tents, and the Eskimos are ready to move inland in search of the food the new season brings: migrating birds, fish, and – above all – the caribou herds.

For those who remain on the coast, the sea is still a prolific provider. As the sea ice breaks up, seals bask at the edges of the floes. They can be hunted here or from kayaks. In Alaska the first whales are sighted. Among the Eskimo, strict tabus exist prohibiting the use of the same weapons and equipment for hunting land and sea animals; these, together with customs like the Alaskan one of giving back the whale's skull (containing its soul) to the sea to ensure the return of more whales, reflect the hunters' respect for the wild animals on which their lives depend.

September sees the first flurries of snow and October the first heavy falls. Inland and coastal Eskimos prepare their winter quarters and by November they are settled in to their snow or sod and stone houses, warmed by lamps of caribou tallow or blubber. There are still some caribou to be hunted inland in the winter and foxes and Arctic hare to be trapped. The coastal Eskimos depend on the seals but they can also fall back on cached food.

Autumn (October–early November)
The first heavy snowfalls. Lakes freeze. The sun sets earlier. Inland Eskimos hunt caribou.

Early winter (late November–December)
The Eskimos are in their sod or snow houses. Seal and walrus are hunted from the ice edge.

Late winter (January–February)
This is the darkest and coldest time. Eskimos harpoon seal at breathing holes and trap foxes.

A land of plenty

To the *Qallunaat* (Whites or southerners), the lands and seas of the Arctic seem desolate, but the Eskimos know that they support a great variety of wild life and they have learnt to trap, hunt and gather everything that is edible or useful there. Arctic weather can make their task incredibly difficult but it also has advantages: freezing temperatures allow food to be preserved for long periods; melted snow can be drunk when rivers and lakes are frozen; cold weather is good for sledge travel.

The majority of Eskimos live on the coast, where seals provide them with food all the year round as well as skins for clothing and tents, and bones for weapons and utensils. They hunt walrus, whales and polar bears, fish, shoot sea birds and collect eggs.

In summer, the sea ice breaks up and the Eskimos take to their kayaks to hunt. Or they trek inland to the tundra to intercept the migrating herds of caribou, which they hunt for meat and for their warm skins. Inland, the summer brings Canada and Snow geese and ptarmigan. Shoals of salmon and char, moving up the rivers from the sea, are trapped and speared in large numbers and some are cached for the winter.

Cliff birds
In May and June, gulls, kittiwakes and guillemots arrive in the Arctic to breed, sometimes forming huge colonies on the cliffs. Their eggs make a protein-rich addition to Eskimo diet. A special delicacy, a *giviak*, is made by stuffing a sealskin with little auks and leaving the whole thing to mature through the summer.

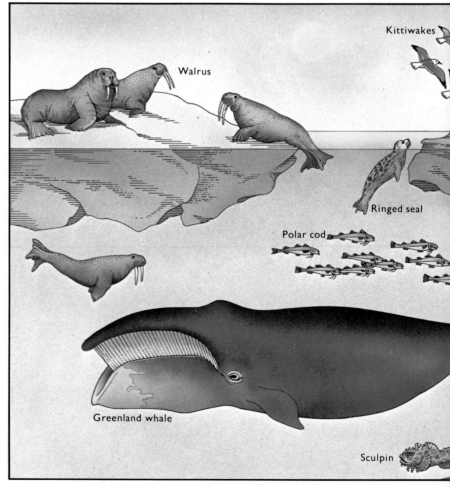

Walrus

Kittiwakes

Ringed seal

Polar cod

Greenland whale

Sculpin

Life on the tundra

The tundra is dotted with lakes, criss-crossed with rivers and covered with low, sparse vegetation: mosses and lichens and species of dwarf willow. In summer, it is marshy, alive with insects, geese, ducks, ptarmigan, Arctic hare, ermine, lemming, musk-oxen and caribou.

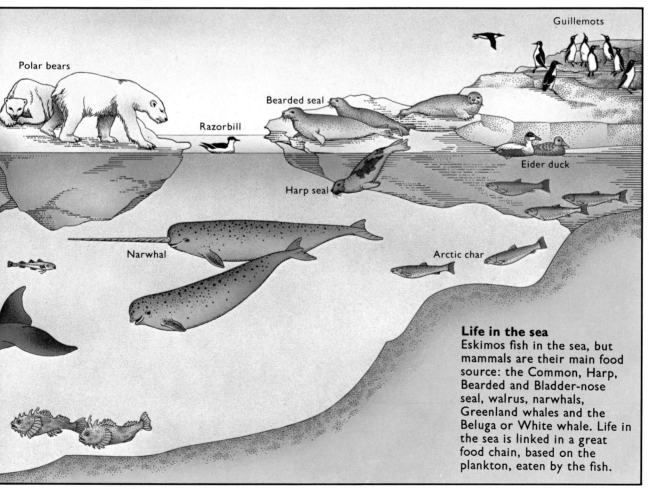

Guillemots

Polar bears

Bearded seal

Razorbill

Eider duck

Harp seal

Narwhal

Arctic char

Life in the sea

Eskimos fish in the sea, but mammals are their main food source: the Common, Harp, Bearded and Bladder-nose seal, walrus, narwhals, Greenland whales and the Beluga or White whale. Life in the sea is linked in a great food chain, based on the plankton, eaten by the fish.

Igloos

Windows for winter houses
Windows of stone houses are made from the bladders or wind-pipes of seals sewn together. For snow houses, a slab of ice is used.

The igloo, or snow house, is probably the best-known feature of Arctic life. Yet it is not built universally among the Eskimo and, where it is found, is more often used as a travelling lodge than as a permanent home. In Eskimo, 'igloo' just means 'a dwelling'; there are special words for the stone and turf house of winter (*quarmak*) and the skin tent of summer (*tupiq*), as well as for the snow house (*igluvigak*).

Driftwood is found in some areas but generally the Eskimos have to make use of other materials for their houses: stone, bone, ivory, turf and snow. Most of the coastal Eskimos build stone and sod winter homes. They cut the turf from the top layer of ground before it freezes in the winter. In many places the sides of these buildings are often reinforced or roofed with the curving ribs of whales. Stones and turf are packed thickly and tightly around this framework. The final shape of the house is a rough dome or a low, flat-roofed square.

The entrances of the stone and sod and snow houses are similar: low, roofed tunnels, sunk lower than the floor of the house proper, to trap cold air. You have to crawl on hands and knees to get in. Both types of house gain extra insulation from every new, blanketing snowfall and both are occasionally lined or given a ceiling with skins.

Winter village life
Leaving their stone and sod houses for the cold air outside, these Greenland Eskimos are preparing for a hunting trip, hoping to catch enough food for the winter ahead.

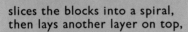
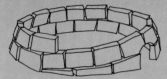
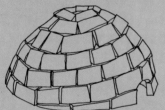
Snow houses are quite effective as permanent dwellings – as long as the weather remains freezing and they do not melt. Inside they are warmed by soapstone lamps filled with blubber or (less efficient) caribou tallow, with floating moss wicks. The lamps are used for cooking and drying clothes as well as heating and are carefully regulated by the woman of the house so that they burn without smoking.

Heat from the lamps and from the bodies inside, makes the inner surface of the snow house walls drip, but the moisture runs down the walls where it quickly re-freezes, forming an inner coating of ice. It is often warm enough inside the house for the people to go around half-naked, in spite of icy temperatures outside.

Snow and sod houses are built by men, with the aid of the women, who help to cover the whole structure with a vital layer of snow for extra insulation. The skin tents of summer are entirely the women's responsibility, they usually lash together the poles as well as making and maintaining the covering of skins. In whaling areas, whalebone supports are used as poles; in other places they may be made of driftwood bound together with bits of walrus and seal bone. The sealskin or caribou hide covers are kept in place by heavy stones placed in a ring round the base where the edges of the skins rest on the ground.

Snow goggles
Snow goggles of ivory or wood, with small slits to see through, exclude snow glare.

A matter of life and death

Warm, hard-wearing clothing is a matter of life or death in the Arctic. Although the clothes of many Eskimo groups are very handsome, their appearance is of minor importance. What matters is that they keep their wearers alive in sub-zero temperatures.

The best way to keep warm is to trap a layer of air between the body and the freezing cold outside. In order to do this, Eskimo clothes are loose and consist of layers. If the clothes were tight, the wearer would sweat and the damp clothes would freeze as soon as they were taken off. Eskimos have never woven clothes – they can depend on the skins of the animals they hunt to provide them with the best protective clothing.

Patterns vary from one region to another but everywhere, in winter, the rule is to wear two layers of caribou skin garments. The outer layer has the fur facing out, and the undergarment has the fur turned in against the skin. A very small number of Eskimo groups who do not have access to caribou, like the Belcher Islanders, wear clothes made of bird skins, especially eider duck.

The top outer garment, the *parka*, is loose enough for a hunter caught in a blizzard to draw his arms inside and hold them against his body for extra warmth.

Wolverine trimming
The only fur on which the breath does not freeze.

Sealskin jacket
The loose top coat, or parka, worn by the hunter is made of sealskin with the fur side outwards. An inner sealskin parka is worn underneath with the fur turned in next to the skin.

Boots and socks
The knee-length inner boots or socks (kamiks), lined with soft moss for warmth, are made of sealskin in summer and caribou in winter. On top are outer boots of the same material. In the coldest weather a third pair of ankle-length bootees of caribou hide may be worn.

A Bering Strait Eskimo wearing a jacket made from eider duck skins

A Greenland woman wearing sealskin boots, trousers and jacket

A Copper Eskimo woman wearing decorated sealskin clothing, unique to the area around Coronation Gulf

Travel in the Arctic

Like all hunting peoples, Eskimos have to travel to make sure of a steady supply of food. In winter, in all but the coldest, stormiest weather the Eskimos can use their dog sledges on the thick, expansive sea ice. Most of the inland bays of the jagged Arctic coast become highways now and even wide stretches of sea ice can be crossed safely. In some places, however, the ice has great pressure ridges, formed when rough seas and high tides break and disturb the sheets of new ice as they form. In these conditions, sledging is very hazardous.

Sledges are made of wood, or pieces of bone or ivory lashed together – occasionally, when no other materials are available, the runners can even be made of tightly rolled sealskin, or frozen fish, wetted and patted into shape. A row of slats is lashed across two stout runners to form a narrow platform between 1·5 and 6 metres long. Sledges are pulled by the Eskimo dogs, hardy animals, who usually sleep outside, backs to the wind, tails curled round their

The woman's boat
Eskimo women row the umiak when it is used as a cargo boat and carries the whole family, dogs and all their possessions.

The kayak
The wood or bone frame of this light, narrow boat is covered with waterproof sealskin. The kayaker sits on a piece of caribou to protect him from cold.

noses to keep in as much body heat as possible. They can be wild but are firmly controlled by an experienced driver who can pick out a single dog from a team and flick it on the ear with his 4·5-metre sealskin whip. The size of a dog team varies with the load to be carried, availability of food supplies and dogs, and the length of the journey. The Netsilik Eskimos rarely had more than five dogs to a team; the Iglovik rarely had fewer than ten.

In summer, when the ice melts, the Eskimos travel on foot. The dogs can be used as pack animals – although they sometimes roll on their loads! The Eskimo boats come into their own now. The light, manoeuvrable kayak is used on rivers and lakes to attack the caribou as they splash through them on their summer migrations, and at sea for hunting seal, walrus, Beluga whales and narwhal. The much larger umiak is employed as a cargo boat in most places, but in Greenland and Alaska it is used for hunting Beluga whales.

An Eskimo dog harness

Preparing for a journey
The runners are covered with softened mud (gathered in summer and stored), moulded into shape and allowed to freeze hard. This surface is planed and water is spread over it with a bearskin or rabbit fur brush. The ice freezes, forming a smooth, hard shoeing.

A food for all seasons

Seals are hunted all the year round and almost every part of the animal can be used by the Eskimos. The skin makes boots, jackets, trousers, tents, covers for kayaks, bags and ropes and lines. The thick layer of blubber is used for fuel and stored in sealskin bags for the winter – it fills the soapstone blubber lamps, used for cooking, lighting and heating. Seal sinews are used for sewing and bones for tools, pegs and toggles for harness.

All the meat on a seal can be eaten – only the gall bladder is discarded because of its bitter taste. The meat is eaten boiled or raw. Because they eat raw food – and every part of an animal – Eskimos get essential vitamins that would otherwise be lacking in a diet with virtually no vegetables. Blubber is often eaten raw as an accompaniment to meat or berries. Blood soup is much enjoyed and the seal's intestines, squeezed out, braided and hung to dry, are eaten as a delicacy.

Common seal

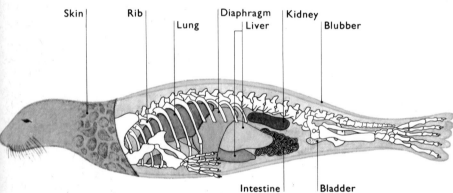

Skin | Rib | Lung | Diaphragm | Liver | Kidney | Blubber | Intestine | Bladder

Wooden knife

Implements for seal hunting
A snow knife is used to cut away snow and ice from the top of the breathing hole. The hunter scrapes gently on the ice with a wooden 'claw' to attract the seal. The harpoon has a loose, barbed head fastened to a short sealskin line, held in the hunter's hand, and a bone, wood or ivory shaft with a bone pick at the end. When the hunter harpoons the seal, the harpoon head pulls loose from the shaft. Bone or ivory pegs plug the seal's wounds.

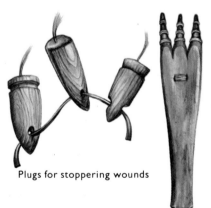

Plugs for stoppering wounds

Wooden 'paw'

Seal harpoon

Methods of seal hunting
Seals are hunted in different ways according to the season of the year. In winter the hunter sits over a breathing hole watching for a movement

of the down indicator. When it moves the seal is underneath and can be harpooned. In winter and early spring leads

open in the sea ice. Nets are put in the water to catch the seals. In late spring and summer

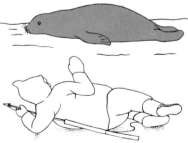

seals bask in the sun. The hunter pretends to be a seal until he is close enough to harpoon it.

The widely distributed Common seal is the one most often killed by the Eskimos, especially in the Central Arctic, but they also hunt the migratory Harp seal, and the Bearded seal; both of these have tough skins which make good ropes, harpoon lines and soles for boots. During the winter, seals can be hunted at their breathing holes, Eskimos keeping long lonely vigils in bone-chilling weather waiting for a kill. In spring they are more plentiful and can be stalked and killed on the ice, or hunted from kayaks.

Among the Central Eskimos, hunters perform a ritual over the first seal they catch. All the hunters gather round the man who has succeeded in harpooning the seal and kneel while he cuts a small hole in its skin and pulls out the liver and a little blubber. He chops them up and they are eaten on the spot by the kneeling hunters. The 'hunters' meal' combines a treat with a show of respect for what nature provides.

Blunt-edged scraper for softening skins

Curing skins

It is usually the Eskimo women who flay the seals. The skins are cleansed of remnants of fat and given their first scraping with a square-ended knife. Then they are washed and scraped again with a curved, one-handed knife. For waterproof clothing, hair is scalded off with boiling water.

Knife with ground stone blade for scraping fat off skins

Hunting the whale

The Thule Eskimos, who spread from Siberia to Greenland in the fifteenth–seventeenth centuries, hunted the huge Greenland whales, but now these animals have been virtually exterminated. The communities in Alaska, where whales are still hunted, are very different from the small mobile hunting groups formed by most Eskimos. These whaling settlements are larger and more permanent – and more highly organised. The most important figures in the whaling communities are the *umialiks*, the owners and steersmen of the big, skin boats, the umiaks.

The elaborate ceremonies that take place before and after a whale hunt, culminating in the spring whaling festival, are evidence of the value of the whales to these communities. The whales begin

First sight of the whale
The umiak crews camp on the edge of the ice to wait for the whales. They are forbidden by custom to use tents. When a whale is sited, the boats are launched and their six-man crews paddle towards it (paddles make less noise than oars). The women watch them from the shore. The umialik himself steers the boat and the harpooner stands in the bows, armed with 1·5 metre-long harpoons, with flint-tipped ivory heads and flint spears for piercing the whale's thin, tough skin and thick blubber.

to appear off the Alaskan coast in June, making their way north through the breaking ice.

When the first whale is sighted, several umiaks put to sea, the harpooners standing ready in the bows with their flint-tipped weapons. It may be possible to harpoon the whale first from the ice; then the boats circle round waiting for it to surface so that they can get close enough to thrust more harpoons in to it. Once the whale has been struck several times, it is slowed down by the lines and the skin or bladder floats to which the harpoon lines are tied. Then a boat can get near enough for the harpooner to try to strike a final deadly blow with his lance. All the boats join to tow the dead whale back to the ice where it can be butchered.

A woman's place

Eskimo men and women divide the work of the community between them. Basically, women take care of the home, food and clothing while men hunt. Marriage is very important in Eskimo society – everyone needs a partner because men and women depend on each other's skills for survival. But if a man and woman do not get on well together they can separate and take new partners until they find someone with whom they can settle down and have children. Children are very much desired, both for themselves and as support for their parents in old age. Eskimo wives are occasionally 'lent': if a hunter is going on a long journey and his own wife is sick, he may take another hunter's wife with him to cook and repair his clothes. Also, women sometimes have two husbands.

Bringing up small children is a woman's task, and so is butchering the animals the hunters bring back, preparing and cooking meals, and making sure that the blubber lamps are filled and their wicks trimmed. Among the inland Eskimos, the women gather brushwood for fires.

But women also sometimes help their husbands to hunt and can drive dog teams and build snow houses if necessary. They fish, either by jiggling a model fish in holes in the ice or, in summer, by spearing fish in the rivers and lakes with leisters (fish spears). They also trap small animals and birds. Women used to do most of the

Tattooing
Tattooing, no longer practised, was once regarded as a mark of feminine beauty. It was usually done at about twelve years of age. A needle and thread dipped in soot was passed under the skin – a very painful process!

Dividing up the whale
Once a whale has been beached, everyone helps to cut it up, and women strip off the blubber. This is a social occasion and the workers stuff pieces of meat and blubber into their mouths as they work. Special parts of the whale go to the crews.

The woman's knife
The *ulu*, or woman's knife, is used for a great variety of purposes by Eskimo women. Now they are made of metal but originally were bone or stone.

Curing and softening skins
In the late spring and summer, Eskimo women sit outside their tents for long hours, their legs straight out in front of them, scraping the blubber and fat from the skins of seal and caribou. After a preliminary scraping, the skins are washed and dried and then scraped again. The tough skins are chewed to soften them. Birdskins are too fragile to be scraped so they are chewed to remove the fat.

Skins are cut into shape for clothing with the semi-circular ulu by pressing the blade on the inside of the skin and rocking it to and fro.

When two caribou skins have been cut to form the back and front pieces of a parka, the two pieces are placed with outsides together and the seams are stitched with a fine bone needle and sinew thread. Eskimo women use several different types of stitching and sew with a skin thimble, which they wear on the forefinger.

fox trapping until this became really vital to Eskimo economy in many places. Then the men, as traditional providers, took over from them.

Perhaps the most important of all an Eskimo woman's tasks is curing skins and making clothes from them. A skilled seamstress is very highly regarded among the Eskimo. A hunter who has to spend many freezing hours waiting for a seal to appear at a breathing hole, or who runs into a blizzard on a long sledge journey, will die if his clothes cannot give him proper protection. Women learn how to cure all the different skins and which ones are most suitable for parkas, or boots, or tents. They know how to cut them out accurately without waste and how to sew them with bone and ivory needles and thread, which they make from dried sinew, so that the seams are firm and watertight. Women are responsible, too, for erecting the summer skin tents as well as making them.

When visitors arrive, the woman of the house will serve them and her husband first, and wait to eat until they have finished. But Eskimo wives are by no means slaves to their husbands. The esteem in which they are held is clear in the Polar Eskimo saying: 'A hunter is what his wife makes him.' To a large extent Eskimo wives are their husbands' partners in a society in which everyone must help one another and co-operate in the struggle for survival.

A brief abundance

High summer in the Arctic is a time of plenty. Herds of migrating caribou thunder over a rich carpet of flowers, heather, grasses and berries. Stomachs and larders are full and the rigours of winter hunting are forgotten. At this time, to vary their diet of venison, the caribou hunters turn to the river. Trout, salmon and char, fish of shallow waters, are the main quarry. They are caught as they battle their way back up river from the sea.

A low, semi-circular weir of stones is built in a shallow stretch of water in the path of the migrating fish. The fish usually arrive in large numbers two or three times a day. When they enter the semi-circle of stones, the mouth of the weir is closed with a few more stones and all the Eskimos, men, women and children, rush yelling and splashing into the water, stabbing to left and right with their leisters. The riot of thrashing fish and stabbing people is very different from the normal, patient, stealthy way in which Eskimos hunt but it produces food for many meals. Fish that are not eaten immediately are gutted and dried on a wooden trestle or cached for the winter.

As autumn advances, the caribou skin tents are taken down. The casual life of the fish camp and the ample diet of caribou, fish and wild berries give place to thoughts of winter. Before they prepare for the cold weather, however, the hunters have a last stab at their fish. They move to the ice which begins to form again on the lakes in autumn. There they lure the fish to the surface at the ice edge by jiggling a model fish in the water. As the prey rises, it is speared with a leister or harpoon and threaded onto lines held in the fishermen's mouths. Once the lakes have iced over completely, the long northern winter has really set in.

The fruits of summer
Edible berries are among the plants which flourish briefly at the end of the summer. Cranberry, bilberry and crowberry are favourites with the Eskimos – sometimes eaten with blubber. The berries provide extra nutrition.

The inland Eskimo

Bird bolas
A bolas with small ivory carvings
is thrown into flocks of birds
to entangle or stun them.

There are inland Eskimos in Alaska, but probably the best known inland group are the Caribou Eskimos, who live west of Hudson Bay on the Barren Grounds. This flat land, with its low hills and wide plains, its rivers and vast interior lakes, is crossed and recrossed by the great herds of migrating caribou. The Eskimos who live here depend entirely on the land for food and shelter and may never see the sea.

The biggest caribou hunts take place in the autumn when the caribou, fat and sleek from their summer feeding, trek south for the winter. The meat and skins gained from these hunts provide the basis of the Eskimos' economy for months – until the caribou return again in the spring.

There are always a few caribou remaining on the tundra in the winter, but not enough for the Eskimos to be able to depend on them for survival. Ptarmigan can be shot and fish caught through holes in the lake ice.

These inland Eskimos are strangers to the coastal culture – and even those who do visit the coast to hunt have not adopted the coastal blubber lamp. The shallow lamps of the Caribou Eskimos burn caribou tallow but they also use fires made from brushwood, gathered from under the snow. Fires cannot be lit in the winter snow houses and if they run out of caribou fat, the people sometimes have only the heat of their bodies to keep them warm.

Caribou are shot with rifles now but formerly short-range bows were used. It was necessary to get close to the shy caribou to be sure of hitting them and the Eskimos devised various ways of approaching the animals. In some areas, two avenues of stone cairns were set up, with tufts of grass, lumps of peat, or birds' wings on top to make them look like people. The avenue was very broad at the end from which the caribou would approach. Women and children, acting as beaters, drove the herd down towards the narrow end, where the hunters were waiting in shelters.

Catching the caribou

The inland Eskimos often try to drive the caribou into lakes using decoys and beaters. Then they can take to their kayaks to spear the slow-swimming animals at close quarters and tow them ashore.

25

A time for relaxation

Eskimo drawing of a dance house

Eskimo drawing of a dance house

Carving in ivory
This small carving, made from narwhal tusk, was once designed to represent the spirit of the whale.

Materials for carving
The doll is made from wood with seal fur trimmings and the grouse, from Greenland, is wood too. The ivory and whalebone bow drill, primarily for making hunting equipment, could also be used for carvings. The top part was put in the mouth, the drill placed against the carving and made to rotate by moving the bow attached to the string backwards and forwards.

Like many hunting people who spend long, solitary hours in the search for food, the Eskimos love to gather together for feasts and celebrations when they can. Autumn, before the ice is firm enough to hunt on, is a time for relaxing: for making and mending hunting equipment, for cutting out and sewing winter clothes – and for celebrating with games and dancing. Alaskan Eskimo men often spend all day in the *kazigi*, the men's dance houses, working on their hunting weapons or carving.

Eskimo carvings are most often of dolls or small replicas of marine animals – originally designed to encourage the animals to visit the winter hunting sites. The carvings are of antler, bone, ivory or soapstone and in the past were produced with tools made from the same materials. Ivory and bone could be worked with the bow drills which were primarily used to make holes in sledges or harpoons. Today, Eskimos are encouraged to carve on a commercial scale and they use metal tools for their work.

String games, using sealskin string to make figures and animals, are a popular amusement, and a dice-like game, with little models of people and animals instead of dice, is played on a board. More strenuous games of physical skill and strength, like wrestling, buffets, weight-lifting, jumping or football are widely played. Sometimes Alaskan Eskimos arrange competitions between kazigis.

Eskimo dancing, carried out to the sound of chanting and the striking of a tambourine-like drum (the only Eskimo musical instrument), varies in style from one region to another. In the western Arctic, the dances tend to be elaborate and ritualised while in the east they are much freer and more spontaneous. The men's dances are more vigorous than the women's, the hunters acting out dramatic events like bear hunts. Women's dancing consists of a rhythmical swaying of the top half of the body with very little movement of the feet.

Singing, and especially narrative songs, are features of the autumn entertainments and are usually performed by Eskimo men – the women act as a chorus. The stories, often told by the shamans, or wise men, are traditional legends about the Eskimos in the past and about animals, birds and spirits. They are strikingly similar from Greenland to Siberia. Individual songs, rich in metaphor, in special shamanistic language, are part of the spoken poetry of the Eskimos and express their deep feelings about the world they know and love.

Games

Eskimos are skilful at twisting strips of sealskin into figures and animals: right is a representation of a deer. A game similar to dice is played with small bone figures of birds and people which are shaken in the hand and thrown on a board.

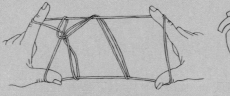

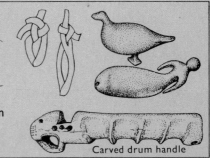

Intricate knots made from sealskin serve not only as a game, but practice for when out hunting.

Carved drum handle

Drumming and dancing

Drumming and dancing are performed by all Eskimos, although the style of the dancing varies from one region to another. This scene is inside a Greenland dance house. Inland Eskimos build extra-large snow houses for dances. It is warm enough inside for the Eskimos to go around half-naked.

The freedom of childhood

Childhood is a time of freedom and play for Eskimos – but many of the games are preparation for the kind of work they will do as adults. Girls play at scraping skins and boys at shooting with bows and arrows and hunting seal. Children are almost never punished. Although they may be made to feel ashamed by other children or adults when they have behaved badly, they are virtually never struck or scolded.

In the old days, new-born girl babies were occasionally killed in times of hardship. But Eskimo parents usually treat their children very affectionately – feeding them the best bits of food and spending hours carving toys and making games for them. Families who have no children adopt them and orphans are taken in by other families. Adopted children are almost always treated with as much love and care as natural offspring.

One of the ways in which parents showed their love for their children in the past was by giving them amulets: charms designed

Ball and whip game
A sealskin ball, stuffed with moss, and trimmed with skin strips, is hit with a sealskin whip.

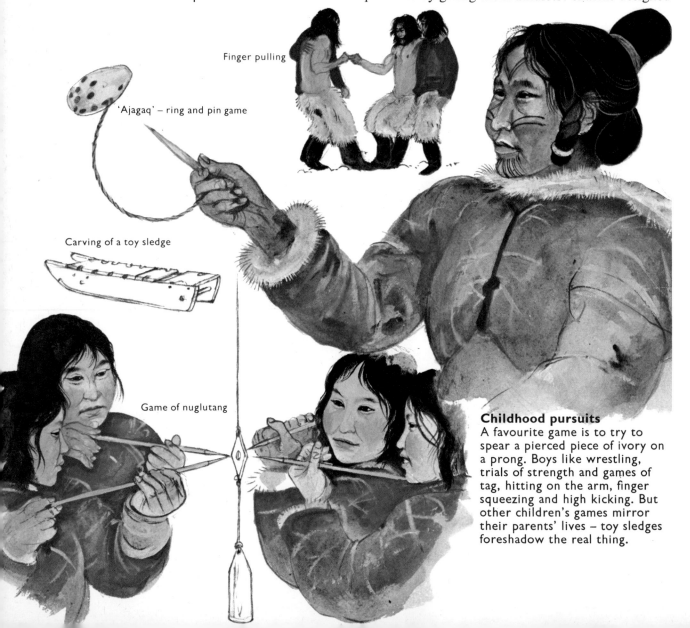

Finger pulling

'Ajagaq' – ring and pin game

Carving of a toy sledge

Game of nuglutang

Childhood pursuits
A favourite game is to try to spear a pierced piece of ivory on a prong. Boys like wrestling, trials of strength and games of tag, hitting on the arm, finger squeezing and high kicking. But other children's games mirror their parents' lives – toy sledges foreshadow the real thing.

Amulets
There are two main types of amulets. Those that are worn from birth are designed to encourage certain qualities in the wearer, like strength or skill in hunting. Feather, bits of skin, fur or claws, bird skulls all represent these attributes.

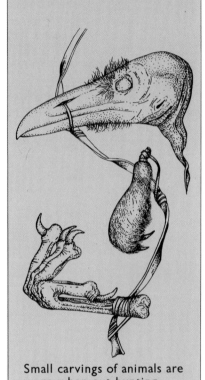

Small carvings of animals are worn when out hunting.

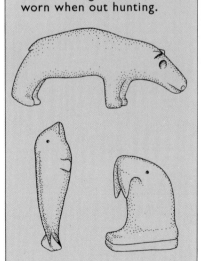

to ward off evil spirits or to ensure good qualities in the possessor. A piece of salmon skin would make a girl a good seamstress; owls' claws would give a boy strong fists. Before the widespread adoption of christianity by the Eskimos, they believed in a teeming spirit world and the use of amulets was one way of appeasing these spirits. The shaman, by going into trances, could contact the spirit world and report to the people what they should do to humour, or drive away, the spirits. Shamans were often called in to advise on naming a new-born baby. The child would be given the name of someone who had died and would inherit the qualities of the dead person.

All the generations were linked in Eskimo society by their traditional way of life – but this is increasingly breaking down with the spread of modern life to the Arctic. Old people are still regarded with respect and affection, however. The tales they tell their grandchildren help the young people to learn the traditions and values of the Inuit. They are a vital link with the world of the real Eskimo and a last repository of old skills and crafts.

When old people fell ill in the past, it was not unknown for them to commit suicide, or be helped to do so, if they felt that life was too much of a burden. With the spread of christianity this practice has vanished. So, too, have the old burial customs. The most common method of burial was to place the corpse, sometimes wrapped in skins, under a cairn of stones. Weapons and implements were sometimes left beside the body for use in another life.

Old age
This old Eskimo man is using a traditional bow-drill – now superseded by modern tools. Old people like him are the last links with the old Eskimo culture, which was technically a stone-age one.

The changing life of Eskimos

The old life of Eskimos as a nomadic, hunting people, dependent on the land and the seasons, has almost vanished. Modern Eskimos are in danger of becoming ordinary Russians, or Canadians, or Americans who happen to be out in the cold – literally and figuratively. They are at a disadvantage in trying to adapt to a culture which is alien to them. Outside pressures on the Eskimos, begun in the last century by traders and missionaries, continued now by oil companies and government agencies in the name of progress, have nothing to do with their traditional life. At least trapping, which the traders encouraged, employed traditional skills; working as a clerk in a government office or driving an oil company truck does not.

The Eskimos survived the first evils of White exploitation – like the murderous epidemics of diseases to which they had no resistance. But now, as commerce and government interfere increasingly in their lives, they are in danger of becoming strangers in their own land.

Eskimos appreciate modern tools and equipment, like high-powered rifles and the snowmobiles which have replaced the old dog sledges, and the kerosene stoves and sewing machines which make home life more comfortable. But they would like to use these things in the context of their old life – one in which they were able to hunt and enjoy 'real' food they caught themselves. It remains to be seen whether any of the old culture can survive the 'benefits' as well as the evils of modern industrialised society in the Arctic.